SLAVERY

during the

REVOLUTIONARY WAR

BY ESTHER PAVAO

Slavery During the Revolutionary War
By Esther Pavao

Published by:

Greatest Stories Ever Told
www.greatest-stories-ever-told.com

P.O. Box 307
Selmer, TN 38375

ISBN, print ed.: 978-0-9888119-80
ISBN, digital ed.: 978-0-9888119-1-1

Preface:

This booklet started as a short work assignment. When my boss (who also happens to be my father-in-law—how cool is that?) asked me to look into a claim that George Washington owned slaves, not only had I never thought to ask whether that was true, but what I pulled up was a shocking revelation to me. And apparently I was not the only one asking questions because some of this information was pretty difficult to track down. Once I started, however, I couldn't stop. I'm not sure if my boss knew how much I loved history, but he figured it out soon enough. He encouraged me to collect the information and then informed me that I was writing it into a booklet which he was going to publish.

I got to spend my work hours poring over biographies, websites, magazines, and letters, tracking down sources for accuracy, and in short, having a total blast.

So about three months later, hours of research, writing, and my inability to shut up about what I was finding (thanks for your patience, honey!), here it is.

Esther

Dedication:
This booklet is dedicated to my big sister.
Your love of history sparked my own.
Thanks.

Slavery During the Revolutionary War

Slavery existed around the world long before the Revolutionary War began. In what was to become the United States of America, it began at some time in the 1500's. By the time the Colonies were established in the 1600's, slavery was accepted as a necessary part of commerce and economic growth throughout Europe.

Every slave-owner was different, so slaves were treated differently from household to household, but the very basis of slavery was unchanging: a slave's life was not his own; his choices were made for him; he had to ask to make basic decisions about his life. At any moment his world could be torn apart; children or spouses could be sold and never seen again.

Stories about slavery in the words of former slaves leave us with no doubt that the practice itself is evil. I have yet to read a defense of slavery that is morally sound *and* logical, and I have yet to find one that isn't monetarily driven.

Slavery, as described by slave-owners, is the natural order of things: convenient and profitable for the owners. George Washington himself owned so much property and so many slaves that he and his family were almost self-sustaining.[1] In cases like this, there would be slaves working in the plantation fields—growing tobacco, sugar cane, cotton, corn, etc.—as well as a number of slaves who kept the household running: cleaning, cooking, sewing, weaving fabric, and

---

[1] Ron Chernow, *Washington: A Life,* (The Penguin Press HC, 2010), 141

waiting on the family. This almost sounds like a charming picture of a rural farm.

Washington was a stern general and slave-owner. He believed good behavior should be rewarded with good treatment and vice versa. He was known to use the whip for soldiers who in any way embarrassed the army. He was a hard worker and expected the same from those beneath him—slave or soldier. Washington was known as a "good" owner because he gave his slaves good housing, medical treatment, clothing, and only used the whip occasionally.

Slavery in the eyes of slaves, however, is not so picturesque...

> "I would ten thousand times rather that my children should be the half-starved paupers of Ireland than to be the most pampered among the slaves of America."[2]

This was written by Harriet Ann Jacobs, a household slave who wrote a book about her trials as a slave in 1861, during the Civil War. The title page of her book bears the quote,

> "Northerners know nothing at all about slavery. They think it is perpetual bondage only. They have no conception of the depth of the *degradation* involved in that word, slavery; if they had, they would never

---

[2] Harriet Ann Jacobs, *Incidents in the Life of a Slave Girl* (Published for the Author, 1861), 49

cease their efforts until so horrible a system was overthrown."

Jacobs attributes this quote to "A Woman of North Carolina," and it sums up the difference in how whites and blacks viewed slavery.

To the slaves, it was not merely the work or the punishment inflicted on them, it was the fact that they were *owned*. They had no say in their lives; they were *possessions*. Some of them were fed well and had comfortable homes, but no *freedom*.

Below are a few comments about slavery by slaves. In my opinion, they are the ones who can give the clearest, most accurate pictures of what slavery was *really* like.

> "... the very first salute I had from them was a violent blow on the head with the fore part of a gun, and at the same time a grasp round the neck. I then had a rope put about my neck, as had all the women in the thicket with me, and were immediately led to my father, who was likewise pinioned and haltered for leading. In this condition we were all led to the camp."[3]

---

[3] Venture Smith, *A Narrative of the Life and Adventures of Venture Smith, a Native of Africa, but Resident above Sixty Years in the United States of America. Related by Himself*, (New London, 1798, reprinted 1835 H.M. Selden, Haddam, Conn., 1896)

"The slave girl is reared in an atmosphere of licentiousness and fear. The lash and the foul talk of her master and his sons are her teachers. When she is fourteen or fifteen, her owner, or his sons, or the overseer, or perhaps all of them, begin to bribe her with presents. If these fail to accomplish their purpose, she is whipped or starved into submission to their will. She may have had religious principles inculcated by some pious mother or grandmother, or some good mistress; she may have a lover, whose good opinion and peace of mind are dear to her heart; or the profligate men who have power over her may be exceedingly odious to her. But resistance is hopeless."[4]

"This same master shot a woman through the head, who had run away and been brought back to him. No one called him to account for it. If a slave resisted being whipped, the bloodhounds were unpacked, and set upon him, to tear his flesh from his bones. The master who did these things was highly educated, and styled a perfect gentleman. He also boasted the name and standing of a Christian."[5]

"I could tell of more slaveholders as cruel as those I have described. They are not exceptions to the general rule. I do not say there are no humane slaveholders. Such characters do exist, notwithstanding the hardening influences around

[4] Jacobs, *op.cit.*
[5] Jacobs, *ibid.*

them. But they are like angels' visits—few and far between."[6]

"I was brought to Missouri when I was six months old, along with my mama, who was a slave owned by a man named Shaw, who had allotted her to a man named Graves. When a slave was allotted, somebody made a down payment and gave a mortgage for the rest. A chattel mortgage. Times don't change, just the merchandise." Sarah Graves, Nodaway Co., MO[7]

"Old Polly whipped my little sister what was only nine months old, ... jus' cause she cry like all babies do, an' it killed my sister ... He was so mean that he never would sell the man an' woman, an' chillen to the same one. He would sell the man here, an' the woman there, an' if they was chillen, he would sell them someplace else." Mary Armstrong, St. Louis, MO[8]

In short, strangers invaded Africa, the Caribbean islands, and the Americas, kidnapped the natives, beat them into submission, bound and shackled them together, and transported them to a foreign country where they would be forced to work the rest of their lives with strange customs, a new language they would have to learn, and where they

---

[6] Jacobs, *ibid.*

[7] Library of Congress: "Slave Narratives"; http://memory.loc.gov/ammem/snhtml/snvoices02.html; accessed Dec. 26, 2012

[8] Missouri State Parks: "Individual Slave Narratives"; http://mostateparks.com/page/58373/individual-slave-narratives; accessed Dec. 26, 2012

would be bought and sold like animals. It's truly barbaric. A large percentage of them died in transit from diseases, dehydration, and physical brutality.

Beatings, whippings, dismemberment, and starvation were common punishments. Runaways were tracked down with dogs. Newspaper ads warned against helping a runaway slave and offered rewards for a slave's return. Many of these ads claim that the slave ran away "with no provocation"—as if just the idea of real freedom weren't tantalizing enough to make them risk their lives. Once tracked down, they could be beaten to death, shot, whipped, or sold.

> "Any slave who attacked a white person faced certain death by hanging or decapitation—death which probably came as blessed relief after first being prodded with red-hot pokers and castrated. Punishments were designed to be hellish so as to terrorize the rest of the captive population into submission. If a slave lifted a hand in resistance, it would promptly be chopped off. Any runaway who returned within a three-month period would have one foot lopped off. If he then ran away a second time, the other foot was amputated. Recidivists [i.e., repeat offenders] might also have their necks fitted with grisly iron collars of sharp, inward-pointing spikes that made it impossible to crawl away...without slashing their own throats in the effort."[9]

[9] Ron Chernow, *Alexander Hamilton*, (The Penguin Press, New York, 2004), 33; brackets mine

There were some kind slave-owners, especially in smaller households with 1 to 5 slaves. It wasn't uncommon to leave slaves their freedom in a will. Many slave-owners got attached to their slaves. James Madison, in response to a letter from a British abolitionist asking questions about slavery in America, explains that the smaller the household, the closer the bond between master and slave.[10]

Slave-owners were terrified that the slaves they oppressed would eventually rise up and fight back. There was a constant fear of insurrection that was always being spoken of and prepared for. Examples were made of slaves who rebelled, made a stand, or tried to fight back. Laws were made that restricted the freedom of freed Negroes.

Overseers frequently checked slave bedrooms and houses for weapons. They were afraid to let their slaves fraternize with other freed slaves in case they encouraged their own slaves to fight for freedom. Some owners forbade their slaves from learning to read or write in order to avoid their passing messages about revolt. Overall, the oppression was so severe that when the opportunity came for the slaves to fight against their owners, thousands of them jumped at the chance.

---

[10] James Madison, *The Writings of James Madison, comprising his Public Papers and his Private Correspondence, including his numerous letters and documents now for the first time printed,* ed. Gaillard Hunt (New York: G.P. Putnam's Sons, 1900). Vol. 9. Chapter: *ANSWERS TO QUESTIONS CONCERNING SLAVERY. 1 [1823]. mad. Mss. http://oll.libertyfund.org/title/1940/119275; accessed 12 Oct. 2012*

The American Revolutionary War

The beginning of the Revolutionary War affected the entire continent; it was inevitable that it would affect slavery as well. Slaves wanted to fight for their freedom as much as, or perhaps more than, the colonists.

Alexander Hamilton and his close friend John Laurens saw this as an opportunity to recruit for the Patriot cause. They both believed that the abolition of slaves was inseparable from the fight for freedom, and they began to petition the South Carolina legislature to allow them to create battalions of black soldiers.

The idea was that slaves who fought for the patriots would be freed. This effort was perhaps driven more by a desire to end slavery than a desire to win the war.

Hamilton wrote a letter to Laurens discussing their plans, saying,

> "I have not the least doubt that the negroes will make very excellent soldiers with proper management ... I think their want of cultivation (for their natural faculties are probably as good as ours) joined to that habit of subordination which they acquire from a life of servitude will make them sooner become soldiers than our white inhabitants ... The contempt we have been taught to entertain for the blacks makes us fancy

many things that are founded neither in reason nor experience; and an unwillingness to part with property of so valuable a kind will furnish a thousand arguments to show the impracticability or pernicious tendency of a scheme which requires such a sacrifice."[11]

John Jay was president of the South Carolina legislature and a fellow abolitionist, so it would be safe to assume he supported this idea. Even so, it failed. Charleston, SC was the largest slave-trading port in the colonies since Boston Harbor had been shut down following the Boston Tea Party. Fear of insurrection and runaway slaves killed their plan before it took off.

Hamilton and Laurens foresaw that if they didn't recruit the Negroes and offer them their freedom, the British would. They were right. The British Governor stationed in the Colonies, Lord Dunmore, saw his chance and seized it. Lord Dunmore proclaimed that any slaves who ran away and joined the British forces would be freed when the war was over.[12]

This stroke of tactical brilliance paid off. About 3,000 – 4,000 slaves signed their name to what is now called "The Book of Negroes" and joined the Tories.[13] Many more

[11] Ron Chernow, *Alexander Hamilton,* (The Penguin Press, New York, 2004), 121 – Ibid., p.167, letter to John Laurens, September 11, 1779
[12] "Africans in America", http://www.pbs.org
[13] A person supporting the British cause and loyal to the crown (King of Britain). Also called a "Loyalist."

joined and fought even without such a promise, simply wanting to overthrow their current masters.

Perhaps the best known of these is Colonel Tye, or Titus. He ran away from his master at age 22 and joined the British Ethiopian Regiment. He is most famous for his fierce guerrilla tactics and his capture of a rebel militia captain during the Battle of Monmouth.

He gave himself the title "colonel" even though the British army didn't rank black soldiers. He and his small mixed-race band, called the Black Brigade, viciously raided New Jersey, stole clothing and supplies from Patriot homes, and murdered several prominent citizens.

Tye's feats encouraged other slaves to run away to New York, which was being held by the British. He is arguably the most well-known Negro soldier. He later suffered lockjaw, a symptom of tetanus, brought on by a gunshot wound to the wrist which eventually killed him.[14]

We have to admire the genius behind this proclamation, even if it wasn't a new idea. The slaves who responded to the proclamation would be desperate to win the war. They would fight to the death to avoid going back to their former lives, and they would have the chance to fight against their oppressors, possibly face to face. Giving them the chance to fight would swell the British ranks with desperate soldiers willing to do anything to win. An estimated 100,000 African

---

[14] Colonel Tye (1753-1780), http://www.blackpast.org; accessed December, 2012 http://wikipedia.org; accessed December, 2012 "Africans in America," http://www.pbs.org; accessed December, 2012

Americans escaped, died, or were killed during the American Revolution.[15]

The Patriots, however, were afraid of the slaves rising up against them if they held weapons, and so General George Washington barred the Patriot army from recruiting blacks, even previous soldiers. Several months later, however, after Lord Dunmore's proclamation, Washington changed his mind, wrote home, and Congress ratified his decision to allow free blacks to reenlist in the army if they chose to. The number of men dropping out of the army when their enlistments were expired had made him desperate for more recruits. Approximately five thousand blacks joined the army after this.[16]

There was some hypocrisy in blacks fighting for the Patriotic cause. The war was for liberty, but that liberty wasn't extended to the Negroes. When the war was over, except for those slaves who responded to Lord Dunmore's proclamation, the Negroes were still enslaved. The desire for freedom from oppression drove hundreds of slaves to fight, but in the end, most of them were fighting for their oppressors' freedom. The twisted irony here is astounding.

On the other hand, there were some slave-owners who were awakened by the fight for independence and, to their credit, freed their slaves because of it. A popular narrative of this time is of William Whipple, New Hampshire representative and signer of the Declaration of Independence, and his

---

[15] " Africans in America," http://www.pbs.org
[16] Ron Chernow, *Washington: A Life*, (The Penguin Press HC, 2010), 213

personal slave, Prince Whipple.[17] General Whipple freed his slaves because he couldn't reconcile fighting for his own independence and not allowing his slaves the same privilege.[18]

After the war, the Loyalist blacks who could prove that they had served the British side, whose names were in the Book of Negroes, were freed by Lord Dunmore and relocated to Nova Scotia, Jamaica, and Britain.[19] There were a few cases where their owners found them and proved their ownership, and those slaves had to be returned. I'm sure that they didn't receive a warm welcome after running away and fighting against the Patriots. History speaks for itself: when slaves upset their masters, there was punishment.

When telling about runaways, Harriet Ann Jacobs wrote:

"Various were the punishments resorted to. A favorite one was to tie a rope round a man's body, and suspend him from the ground. A fire was kindled over him, from which was suspended a piece of fat pork. As this cooked, the scalding drops of fat continually fell on the bare flesh."

---

[17] It was common for slaves to take on the surnames of their masters or mistresses if they didn't have their own.
[18] Dorothy Mansfield Vaughan, "This Was A Man: A Biography of General William Whipple," (Read by the author at a meeting of the National Society of The Colonial Dames in the State of New Hampshire, 1964) http://www.whipple.org; accessed February 13, 2013
[19] "Revolutionary War," http://www.nps.gov; accessed February 13,2013

It is difficult to believe that punishment would be anything less than brutal for a slave who ran away *and* fought against his owner.

The Founding Fathers

The Founding Fathers were slave-owners too. It is hard indeed to comprehend that the people who wrote the famous line, "we hold these truths to be self-evident, that all men are created equal," owned slaves. As I said at the beginning of this booklet, while we can't imagine living in a world that condones slavery, they called that world home. George Washington, Benjamin Franklin, Thomas Jefferson, James Madison, and Patrick Henry were all signers of the declaration of independence, and they were all slave-owners.

We don't want to believe that our heroes, our icons of liberty, were participants in one of the greatest injustices inflicted on mankind. Even they felt that their war for independence was hypocritical, and said as much:

- Patrick Henry, who is most famous for his quote, "Give me liberty, or give me death!," wrote in a letter, "I am drawn along by the general inconvenience of living without them. I will not–I cannot justify it, however culpable my conduct."

- George Washington wrote to a friend and said, "I can only say that there is not a man living who wishes more sincerely than I do to see a plan adopted for the abolition of [slavery]." Despite this, he owned slaves his entire life, from his father's death when George was 11 until his own death at age 68. His biography by renowned historian Ron Chernow includes a chapter discussing Washington's personality and how it would have affected his slaves. He even says Washington *enjoyed* chasing down runaway slaves and catching them.[20]

- Patrick Henry also wrote, "It is not a little surprising that Christianity ... should encourage a practice so totally repugnant to the first impressions of right and wrong."

- James Madison, in a letter to his father, told a story about his slave who was traveling with him. He concluded that he would have to sell the slave, though "I do not expect to get near the worth of him; but cannot think of punishing him by transportation merely for coveting that liberty for which we have paid the price of so much blood, and have proclaimed so often to be the right, & worthy the pursuit, of every human being." The writings of James Madison leave the impression that he didn't really believe that slavery would end in his lifetime. He is not known for strong abolitionist leanings.

---

[20] Chernow, *op. cit.*, 116

Before we judge too harshly, we must understand that slavery was established long before these men were even born. For centuries, slavery had been a growing part of the economy worldwide, not just in the Colonies. Our Founding Fathers were born into a world that relied on slave labor. It's been said that since slavery was so commonplace, growing a conscience about it could easily have never happened. The fact that they fought slavery at all was extraordinary for their time period.

Every major (and minor) issue in history always has two sides, one fiercely for and one stubbornly against. It seems reasonable to conclude that when slavery was originally instituted, there had to have been someone that fought tooth and nail to oppose it. When has this not been the case?

Even if it were a gradual climb from indentured servants paying debts that escalated to racial separation and then traveling to other continents and kidnapping natives, surely there was a point in history where someone cried, "Enough!" I think the Emancipation Proclamation was decades overdue.

Most of the Founding Fathers made statements against slavery, whether publicly or privately, though most expressed the opinion that it wouldn't end in their lifetime—and behaved accordingly.

Alexander Hamilton, John Jay, and Benjamin Franklin (in his later years), all stood in strong opposition to slavery.

Benjamin Franklin was the first President of the Pennsylvania society for Promoting the Abolition of Slavery, which included Jay and Hamilton. The year he died, he signed a petition for the abolition of all slaves. (He died before he got to see it become a reality.) John Adams never personally owned a slave and is said to have defended them in some cases as a lawyer. He and his wife Abigail Adams believed slavery was evil; however, as a politician "he made no effort to loosen the shackles of those in bondage."[21]

John Jay, as governor of New York, made numerous efforts to push anti-slavery laws. With the help of Alexander Hamilton and a few others, he founded the New York State Society for Promoting the Manumission of Slaves and New York's African Free School. His work, as he puts it, was this: "I purchase slaves, and manumit [free] them at proper ages, and when their faithful services shall have afforded a reasonable retribution." My favorite quote from him regarding his work is, "In my opinion, every man, of every colour and description, has a natural right to freedom, and I shall ever acknowledge myself to be an advocate for the manumission of slaves."[22]

Alexander Hamilton grew up in and around slavery in the Caribbean islands and was always against it and disgusted by it. He did have one slave given to him when he was a child,[23] and there are a few quotes in his letters that suggest

---

[21] John Ferling, *John Adams,*(Holt Paperbacks, 1996) 172
[22] Jay William, *The Life of John Jay: with selections from his correspondence and misc. papers,* (J. & J. Harper, 1833), brackets mine
[23] Ron Chernow, *Alexander Hamilton*, (The Penguin Press, New York, 2004), 23

that he may have had one or two household slaves, but he was an avid abolitionist most of his life. His wife's parents did own slaves, and it is possible they bought slaves for him and Elizabeth Hamilton.

Having read their works and some of their biographies, it seems unlikely to me that they were cruel slave-owners. Fighting for liberty made sympathetic slave-owners of some, and there's no reason to believe the founding fathers were any different.

The Revolutionary war seems to have been the turning point for Franklin who didn't publicly fight slavery until later in his life, after the war. He taught his slaves to read and write and cared very much for some of them. Benjamin Franklin wrote home to his wife:

> "Peter was taken ill with a Fever and Pain in his Side before I got to Newcastle; I had him blooded[24] there, and put him into the Chair, wrapt up warm, as he could not bear the Motion of the Horse, and got him here pretty comfortably. He went immediately to bed and took some Camomile Tea; and this Morning is about again and almost well."

Franklin also requested in his will that Peter and his wife Jemima be freed at his death. Madison is quoted as

---

[24] "Blooding" or "bloodletting" was a common practice. It was drawing a small amount of blood in order to draw out diseases or "bad blood."

instructing an overseer to "treat the Negroes with all the humanity and kindness consistent with their necessary subordination and work."

In letters from these men home to their wives, they recall many stories about their personal slaves, ask about their well-being, and in more than one case, they requested in their wills that those closest to them be freed.

Thomas Jefferson is believed to have fathered one, if not all six, of the children belonging to his slave Sally Hemings. He was home from traveling around 8 or 9 months before all of her children were born, and her children were born with light skin and bore a marked resemblance to Jefferson.[25]

DNA tests on Jefferson's and Hemings' descendants rule out some of the other theories and match at least one of Hemings' children to Jefferson.[26] Some historians believe the claims of Sally Hemings' son Madison Hemings, that he is Jefferson's child, to be true.[27]

Jefferson, like Washington, owned hundreds of slaves. He was raised around slaves all his life. He, like the other Founding Fathers, was anti-slavery for moral reasons, but he was also a man with a large property, large debts, and used

---

[25] James T. Callendar, The Richmond Recorder, 1802, as cited by Ron Chernow, *Alexander Hamilton,* (The Penguin Press, New York, 2004), 662
[26] *Nature* 396, 27-28 (5 November 1998)
[27] "The History of a Secret," http://www.pbs.org/wgbh/pages/frontline/shows/jefferson/cron/; accessed December, 2012; ibid: "Life Among the Lowly", S.F. Wetmore, Pike County Republican, 1873

to a comfortable lifestyle. He may have been against slavery on paper, but in reality, the financial advantages to owning slaves made the final call for him.

Jefferson even suggested to a friend that if he had any cash left, "every farthing of it [should be] laid out in land and negroes, which besides a present support bring a silent profit of from 5. to 10. per cent in this country by the increase in their value." He disliked controversy of any kind, including beating slaves, but he hired overseers to do that work for him. He did pay some of his slaves, but only few. [28]

None of the Founding Fathers lived to see the legal abolition of slavery.

[28] Henry Wiencek, (2012, October), "Master of Monticello," *Smithsonian*, 40-49 & 92-97, brackets mine

The Three-Fifths Compromise

The cost of war had left the country deeply in debt; and although taxation was a highly sensitive subject to the Colonists, it arose as an effective solution to the debt. It also brought up a question on the issue of slavery, which had become a taboo subject during the war in order to preserve the unity.

The North, where most free slaves had chosen to settle, and the South, which was primarily populated by plantation owners who owned numerous slaves, were growing increasingly at odds with each other over the issue of slavery, taxation, and representation in Congress. Should slaves be counted as people or as property when taxing slave-owners?

If they were counted as property, the slave-owners could be taxed for them, meaning the South would pay more taxes than the North. The delegates from the South felt that only free men should pay taxes. Since the freed slaves mostly migrated north, this would tax the northern states more than the South. However, it also meant that because there were more people, there was more representation in Congress for northern states. Anything put to a vote would likely fall in the North's favor.

If they were to be taxed for the slaves, the South argued, they should be able to have that much more representation in congress. The South demanded that they should have one vote for each slave they owned, to be used by the slave's owner. They felt this would rectify the imbalance. The North felt this was unfair to slaves since they didn't get to choose where their vote was cast.

Alexander Hamilton argued:

"Much has been said of the impropriety of representing men who have no will of their own. ... They are men, though degraded to the condition of slavery. They are persons known to the municipal laws of the states which they inhabit, as well as to the laws of nature. But representation and taxation go together. ... Would it be just to impose a singular burden, without conferring some adequate advantage?"

After a long argument, the North conceded three-fifths of a vote for each slave to be used by the slave's owner in order to have more equal representation in Congress. I can't help but find this ironic considering that the catalyst for the Revolutionary War was the issue of "taxation without representation."

In his book, *Negro President: Jefferson and the Slave Power*, Garry Wills, Pulitzer-prize winning author and historian outlines how much this affected which laws were passed. Thomas Jefferson would never have been president if it weren't for the Three-Fifths Compromise. He claims that Jefferson actually had fewer votes than his opponent,

John Adams, but he was the popular candidate for the South. He made it into the office "on the shoulders of slaves."[29]

The Three-Fifths Compromise is commonly misinterpreted. Many take it to believe that the Founding Fathers viewed slaves as three-fifths of a person. They may or may not have viewed their slaves as less than people, but the Three-Fifths Compromise does not imply this.

---

[29] Gary Wills, *Negro President: Jefferson and the Slave Power* (Houghton Mifflin Company, 2003), 2

Understanding the Act for the Gradual Abolition of Slavery

It would have been impossible to vote in a law abolishing slavery without an uproar from the Southern States. An act was submitted before the Pennsylvania legislature that suggested a gradual freeing of slaves over a span of almost 30 years. It outlined an idea that, if it worked, would have gradually freed slaves and given plantation owners and slaveholders the chance to slowly convert their individual enterprises to rely on hired workers instead of slaves.

It was a formal compromise between the abolitionists and the slave-owners, a promise that things were finally changing and, most likely, a chance to procrastinate and draw out slavery for as long as it could be gotten away with. (That last one is a personal opinion; as you won't find that written anywhere in historical documents.)

The cost of laborers versus slaves at that time was explained by Reverend Peter Fontaine in 1757:

> "A common laborer, white or black ... is 1s . sterling or 15d. currency per day; a bungling carpenter, 2s. or 2s. 6d. per day; besides diet and lodging. That is, for a lazy fellow to get wood and water, £19 16s. 3d. current per annum; add to this £7 or £8 more and you have a slave for life."

To put this in modern terms, it cost approximately $10/day, or almost $3,800 a year to hire a laborer. Slaves could cost anywhere from £20 to £80 ($4,100 to $16,300), sometimes more, depending on the age, gender, talents, attractiveness, and physical fitness of a slave.

Rev. Fontaine was pro-slavery, and according to him, it would obviously make more sense to pay the money up front and have the lifelong labor, as opposed to paying daily wages. After a year, the slave's labor would more than pay for the up-front cost. He also makes some pro-slavery arguments in a letter that seem to conflict with his title of reverend, but it wasn't unusual for professed Christians to own slaves.

The Act for the Gradual Abolition of Slavery was passed by the Pennsylvania legislature on March 1, 1780. It was the first act to begin successfully freeing slaves.

The Act did not limit the rights of slave-owners, and those currently in slavery were not freed by it. In summary:

- **Sections 1 and 2** outline the purpose of the Act.

- **Section 3** states that all persons born in the state of Pennsylvania after the Act was passed are no longer slaves or "lifelong servants of any kind."

- In **Section 4**, it goes on to say that even though the children born were not "slaves," they are required to remain in the service of their owners as a type of indentured servant or apprentice until that child was 28 years old. Indentured servants were granted small privileges in court and had some rights that slaves didn't, so this was an improvement.

- **Section 5** requires all slave-owners to register their slaves annually—names, ages, and etc.—in order to enforce the freeing of the slaves at age 28 and to keep track of which ones had already been freed. If owners failed to register their slaves, they would have to free them by default.

- **Section 6** reinforces that as soon as the slaves reach 28, owners were required to give them a bill of sale and free them.

- **Section 7** gives slave children (the indentured) the same rights in a court of law as other indentured servants, although as slaves or as Negroes, they were still not allowed to testify against whites.

- **Section 8** promises reimbursement for slave-owners whose slaves were given the death sentence in court, based on the jury's evaluation of the slave's worth.

- **Section 9** covers the punishment for harboring or assisting runaway slaves.

- **Section 10** banned all future slavery and protected every freed man from ever being enslaved again, but excluded visitors to the state or anyone staying less than 6 months. Some people did take advantage of this section by leaving every 6 months and coming back.

- **Section 11** freed slaves who had run away and been missing for more than 5 years, while allowing owners to recover slaves missing during this time period.

- **Sections 12 and 13** make longer forms of indentured servitude illegal, regardless of laws in other states.

- **Section 14** repeals any older laws inconsistent with this new law.

An amendment was made in 1788 to close the loophole accidentally left in Section 10. Slave-owners would transport pregnant slaves over the state line to give birth. The baby was then "legally born into slavery" since the Act was for Pennsylvania only. They also would "move," so that their residence in Pennsylvania was under six months, in order to subvert the law.

However, the 1788 amendment was overruled as unconstitutional due to some conflicting statements. Far from the 28 years planned, the last slaves in Pennsylvania weren't freed until 1847, sixty-seven years later.

In his second term of presidency, Thomas Jefferson signed an act prohibiting the import and export of slaves into the U.S. This stopped the transatlantic slave trade, and now it was time to address the issue of the slaves who were not covered under the Gradual Act.

James Madison wrote "The general emancipation of slaves ought to be 1. gradual. 2. equitable & satisfactory to the individuals immediately concerned. 3. consistent with the existing & durable prejudices of the nation." The prevalent belief of the time was that blacks and whites couldn't live in the same place. The prejudices were too high and the hatred built up after years of enslavement would create insurmountable friction.

Madison goes on to suggest segregation of blacks and whites, even that all free blacks should be transported back to Africa. The letter suggests that many authority figures agree with this plan and even those who doubted its success "wished to find themselves in an error." Very few people believed that blacks and whites were compatible, and even some abolitionists believed that was the best plan.

Other states began to adopt the Act for the Gradual Abolition of Slavery. A slave sued for his freedom and won in Massachusetts. Apparently, this happened frequently or at least was becoming more and more common. John Adams commented, "I never knew a Jury, by a Verdict to determine a Negro to be a slave—they always found them free." Several states, including Massachusetts, skipped the gradual and outlawed slavery entirely.

The Act, though it was a long process, did succeed in legally kick-starting the abolition of slavery. The Southern states put up quite a fight, and effectively slowed things down.

Things were far from over at the abolition of legal slavery. A lifestyle that's been in practice for centuries doesn't vanish with one document being signed. Aside from people fighting the law in court and undercover, the racial separation didn't end. Freed Negroes were not allowed certain jobs, had separate hotels, restaurants, public transportation, drinking fountains, park benches, and neighborhoods.

The Emancipation Proclamation

If the Act had worked, we might not have had the Civil War. The Civil War wasn't originally about slavery, although the issue of slavery was a large cause in starting the war. When the Emancipation Proclamation was signed by Abraham Lincoln in 1863 during the Civil War, it raised hope in some.

Since it didn't really apply to all of the states, it didn't finish the job either. It had a very similar effect that Lord Dunmore's proclamation had before the Revolutionary War. It freed the slaves in the states that had seceded from the Union and encouraged them to fight with the Union against the Confederacy, but it didn't free the slaves in the Union.

The Proclamation changed the focus of the war and gave the Union the encouragement, if slightly false, that they were now fighting a "moral war," rather than just trying to reunite the country. Britain, who had been supporting the Confederates, was forced to pull out as they had already passed their own laws against slavery, and fighting with the Confederates was now viewed as "pro-slavery."

The Confederacy lost support and the Union gained it. The Emancipation Proclamation was a political move more than anything else.

The Thirteenth Amendment

Several bills were presented to Congress to finalize the abolition of slavery. President Abraham Lincoln helped push the constitutional amendment that was a combination of several versions which had been, thus far, unsuccessful. The Senate voted, and the House voted. The bill finally passed. Slavery was officially made illegal by the Thirteenth Amendment to the Constitution in December of 1865.

Twenty-seven of thirty-six states ratified the Amendment in 1865. Iowa and New Jersey signed in 1866, Texas in 1870. There was quite a wait in getting the other states that originally rejected the Amendment to sign it, but they eventually did. Delaware signed in 1901 and Kentucky finally signed in 1976.

Mississippi was the last state to ratify the Amendment in 1995. (No, that's not a typo.) Originally, they were offended that they would not be compensated for the loss of their slaves and refused to sign. The signing that finally came about 130 years after the amendment was originally proposed is attributed to a Texas legislature clerk who noticed the missing state and wrote to Congress. Mississippi voted to ratify, although as of 2010, they had not notified the US Archivist, making the ratification unofficial. [30]

---

[30] While this booklet was being published, Mississippi notified the US Archivist of their vote, and on February 18, 2013, ABC News published an article announcing that Mississippi had become the 50th state to ratify the Thirteenth Amendment. "Miss. Officially Abolishes Slavery," http://abcnews.go.com/m/blogEntry?id=18533376; accessed February 19, 2013

The Thirteenth Amendment marked the *legal* end of slavery. It was hardly the end of slavery or the end of the blacks' fight for freedom. The idea that blacks and whites were neither equal nor compatible carried on, and that mental battle took much longer to overcome. That's another story.

As long as there are human beings on this planet, there will always be those who oppress and take advantage of others. There will always be those who try to wriggle out of the laws and those who outright defy them. There is still human trafficking today, in the twenty-first century. But as long as there is evil in the world, there will also be those who fight against it. This is, and always has been, worth the fight.

www.ingramcontent.com/pod-product-compliance
Lightning Source LLC
Chambersburg PA
CBHW060043040426

42331CB00032B/2254